MW00803465

# INLAND WATER
## *Habitats*

By **Barbara Taylor**

GARETH**STEVENS**

GS

P U B L I S H I N G

A Member of the WRC Media Family of Companies

**Please visit our web site at: www.garethstevens.com**
**For a free color catalog describing Gareth Stevens Publishing's**
**list of high-quality books and multimedia programs,**
**call 1-800-542-2595 or 1-800-387-3178 (Canada).**
**Gareth Stevens Publishing's fax: (414) 332-3567.**

**Library of Congress Cataloging-in-Publication Data**

Taylor, Barbara, 1954-
  Inland water habitats / Barbara Taylor. – North American ed.
     p. cm. — (Exploring habitats)
  Includes bibliographical references and index.
  ISBN-10: 0-8368-7254-1 – ISBN-13: 978-0-8368-7254-5 (lib. bdg.)
  1. Wetlands—Juvenile literature.  2. Wetland ecology—Juvenile literature.
3. Freshwater ecology—Juvenile literature.  I. Title.  II. Series.
QH87.3.T39    2006
578.768—dc22                              2006044328

This North American edition first published in 2007 by
**Gareth Stevens Publishing**
A Member of the WRC Media Family of Companies
330 West Olive Street, Suite 100
Milwaukee, WI 53212 USA

This U.S. edition copyright © 2007 by Gareth Stevens, Inc. Original edition
copyright © 2002 by ticktock Entertainment Ltd. First published in Great
Britain in 1999 by ticktock Publishing Ltd., Unit 2, Orchard Business Centre,
North Farm Road, Tunbridge Wells, Kent, TN2 3XF.

Gareth Stevens editor: Richard Hantula
Gareth Stevens designer: Charlie Dahl
Gareth Stevens managing editor: Mark J. Sachner
Gareth Stevens art direction: Tammy West
Gareth Stevens production: Jessica Morris

Picture Credits: t=top, b=bottom, c=centre, l=left, r=right, OFC=outside
front cover, OBC=outside back cover, IFC=inside front cover

Oxford Scientific Films; 2ct, 2/3c, 3br, 3tr, 4tl, 4bl, 4/5t, 5cb, 6tl, 7br, 7c, 7cr,
8ct, 8/9c, 9t, 10bl, 10ct, 11cl, 12br, 13c, 16bl, 16/17t, 16/17b, 17cr, 17br, 18bl,
18tl, 19br, 19tr, 20/21t, 20/21b, 21cb, 22tl, 22c, 23b, 23tl, 23tr, 24cl, 24/25 (main
pic), 25tr, 26/27b, 28ct, 30b, 30l, 30/31cb. Planet Earth Pictures; 24tl. Science
Photo Library; 9b. Still Pictures; 6/7t, 8l, 12/13t. Tony Stone; OFC (main pic),
OFC (inset pic) &12l, OBC & 28/29 (main pic), OBC & 31br, IFC & 20tl, 2l, 3cr,
5cr, 10/11c, 12l, 13tr, 13br, 14bl, 14tl, 14c, 14/15c, 15br, 15r, 18/19, 18/19cb,
21c, 22bl, 24/25t, 26l, 27tr, 27c, 28bl, 28/29b, 28/29t, 30/31t, 31cr, 31b.

Every effort has been made to trace the copyright holders and we apologize in
advance for any unintentional omissions. We would be pleased to insert the
appropriate acknowledgement in any subsequent edition of this publication.

Printed in the United States of America

1 2 3 4 5 6 7 8 9 10 09 08 07 06

# CONTENTS

**RIVER HUNTER**

The adaptable raccoon (*left*) is a survivor and eats almost anything, including fish, crayfish, and frogs. It catches its food from the water with its long, sensitive fingers.

# A WORLD OF WATER

The still, smooth water of lakes and ponds; the sparkling white water of rushing rivers and bubbling streams; the muddy, smelly water of swamps, marshes, and bogs – all these water worlds are rich treasure chests of hidden wildlife. They are fragile, ever-changing places that provide plenty of food and shelter, especially for the young of animals such as insects and fish. Millions of birds nest and feed in these habitats alongside spectacular predators, such as alligators and tigers. Water is a perfect life-support system for the cells of living creatures, which are made of roughly 70 percent water. Water contains, in dissolved form, oxygen for breathing and carbon dioxide for water plants to make their food. It also protects its inhabitants from wide swings in temperature because it heats up and cools down more slowly than the air.

## FOOD ECHOES

Freshwater species of dolphin, such as these Amazon river dolphins (*above*), are almost blind because they don't need their eyes to find food in the cloudy, muddy river waters. Instead, they use echolocation – sending out high-pitched sounds and waiting for the echoes to bounce back from fish. The echoes tell them the shape of objects and how near they are.

## TOO MUCH WATER

Aquatic plants and animals must have ways of preventing too much water from getting inside their bodies. Water lilies, such as these massive Amazon lilies (*left*), have an extra tough, waxy coating on the upper surface of their leaves, and the water runs off them. Their leaves are supported by the water and float on the surface, making good sunbathing platforms.

## HIDDEN DANGER

The strong jaws of the alligator snapping turtle (*left*) could easily bite off your finger. Luckily, it prefers to eat fish, luring them into its mouth with a built-in wriggly worm on its tongue. There are 200 or so species of freshwater turtles lurking at the bottom of lakes, rivers, and swamps. They can stay submerged for long periods, and some hibernate underwater for weeks at a time.

## WETLAND PEOPLES

Many people live near rivers, lakes, and swamps so they can use them for water, food, and transportation. In this floating market in Thailand (*right*), people sell their fruit, vegetables, and other produce from boats because the houses have canals of water flowing past them instead of roads. Waterways all over the world provide vital links for trade and transportation.

## SNORKELS, AQUALUNGS, AND GILLS

One of the most important factors in the life of aquatic animals is their oxygen supply. Hanging upside down from the surface of the water, mosquito larvae (*left*) take in oxygen from the air through a "snorkel" at the rear end of the body. Other animals obtain oxygen through methods that include the aqualungs – bubbles of air – carried underwater by diving beetles, and the gills of fish, tadpoles, and damselfly larvae. Gills allow oxygen from the water to diffuse directly into the animal's body.

## SUPER DIVER

In fast-flowing water and strong currents, many animals and plants have adaptations that stop them from being swept away. The torrent duck (*above*) is completely at home diving into the foaming, rushing waters of rivers in South America's Andes Mountains to look for insect larvae to eat. The duck uses sharp spurs under its wings to cling to slippery rocks while balancing and steering with its stiff tail. Its large webbed feet make it a powerful swimmer.

# WETLANDS OF THE WORLD

## THE AMAZON RIVER

The Amazon is the second-longest river in the world. It and its tributaries hold about a fifth of the Earth's freshwater. About 2,000 species of fish live in the Amazon, as well as many reptiles, such as caimans and anacondas, and mammals such as the Amazonian manatee. When the Amazon floods (*above*), its waters create a unique area of flooded forest the size of England. In the Amazonian lowlands, the swamp forest, called igapo, is flooded for four to seven months of the year up to a height of 40 feet (12 meters).

**W**etlands cover about 6 percent of the Earth's land surface, ranging from soggy peat bogs to vast flooded forests called swamps. They are found all over the world wherever there is heavy rainfall or where water stays on the surface because it cannot drain away through frozen soil or through impermeable rocks. Wetlands occur in every type of climate, including the frozen Arctic tundra; the hot, humid tropical rain forest; and the temperate regions in between. The Okavango Delta wetland wilderness even survives among the sands of the Kalahari Desert. Wetlands are often found along coasts, such as the mangrove swamps of tropical coasts or the salt marshes of river estuaries. Huge areas of wetland occur on the lands drained by giant rivers. Wetlands are always changing as lakes and ponds dry up or fill in with plants, and salt marshes or mangrove swamps gradually extend out to sea.

## LAKE BAIKAL

Lake Baikal (*right*) in Siberia is the deepest and oldest freshwater lake in the world. At least 25 million years old, it is bigger in area than Belgium and contains the world's largest volume of surface freshwater – more than North America's five Great Lakes put together. Baikal has a wide variety of unique wildlife. Over 1,000 of the species that live there are found nowhere else in the world.

## THE CAMARGUE

The famous white Camargue horses (*left*) live in the salty marshes and shallow lagoons of the wetland called the Camargue, in the Rhône River delta in France. The horses eat a lot of marsh reeds, thereby blocking the reeds' spread across areas of free water. Keeping the water free of reeds is essential for tens of thousands of swans, ducks, and geese, as the waters provide food, winter homes, and resting places during their migration.

## MALAYSIAN MANGROVES

Mangrove swamps (*left*) fringe the coasts of Malaysia and other tropical countries. The sticky, squelchy mud is held together by mangrove trees' characteristic dense arching roots. There is little oxygen in the mud, so the mangroves draw it in directly from the air through their roots. A whole army of creatures lives in and on the rich mud of mangrove swamps.

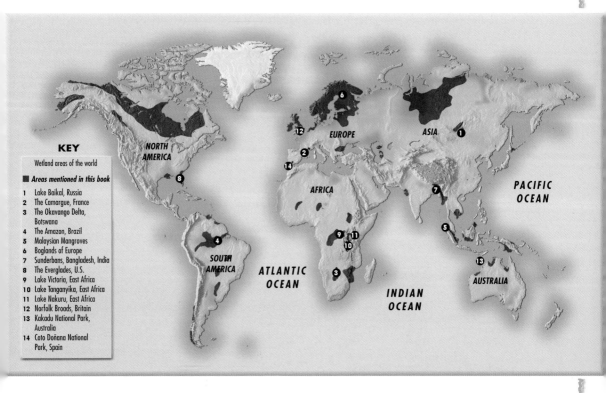

KEY

Wetland areas of the world

■ *Areas mentioned in this book*

1   Lake Baikal, Russia
2   The Camargue, France
3   The Okavango Delta, Botswana
4   The Amazon, Brazil
5   Malaysian Mangroves
6   Boglands of Europe
7   Sunderbans, Bangladesh, India
8   The Everglades, U.S.
9   Lake Victoria, East Africa
10  Lake Tanganyika, East Africa
11  Lake Nakuru, East Africa
12  Norfolk Broads, Britain
13  Kakadu National Park, Australia
14  Coto Doñana National Park, Spain

NORTH AMERICA

SOUTH AMERICA

ATLANTIC OCEAN

EUROPE

AFRICA

ASIA

PACIFIC OCEAN

INDIAN OCEAN

AUSTRALIA

## THE OKAVANGO DELTA

Covering as much as 7,700 square miles (20,000 sq kilometers) of the Kalahari Desert in Botswana, the Okavango Delta (*right*) provides a spectacular oasis for wildlife. It is home to hippopotamuses, crocodiles, lechwe, sitatungas, and thousands of waterbirds, such as ducks, geese, herons, ibises, and fish eagles. In the dry season, desert antelope mingle with wetland species such as waterbuck.

## WETLAND PLANTS

**F**rom algae, mosses, and water lilies to reeds, grasses, and trees – hundreds of flowering and nonflowering plants grow well in wetlands. The water supports the weight of the plant, so there is no need for water plants to have strong stems. Water and nutrients float all around them in the water, so the roots of water plants tend to be small and either float freely or anchor the plant in the mud. In addition, water plants do not have to survive such extreme temperatures as land plants. There are, however, some disadvantages. Oxygen and light may be hard to come by, and flowering and seed production can be difficult, especially in times of flood or drought.

### AIR PLANTS

The silvery bubbles along the leaves of this Canadian pondweed (*above*) are bubbles of oxygen. It is given off as a by-product when the plant makes its food from water and carbon dioxide through photosynthesis. The plant's leaves take in carbon dioxide directly from the water. Because photosynthesis makes use of the Sun's energy, there are more bubbles on sunny days. Canadian pondweed provides oxygen for plants and animals to breathe, but it spreads quickly and can choke other plants.

### WATER POLLINATION

A few plants, such as ribbon weed, rely on water for pollination. This is a more risky process than pollination by insects.

**1.** *Ripe male flowers float up to the surface of the water. They have a bubble of air inside them to help them float.*

**2.** *Male flowers are pushed along by the wind and water currents, and then slide down into the female flower.*

**3.** *Once the female flower has been pollinated, the flower stalk pulls it back under the water.*

**4.** *Under the water, the pollinated flower ripens into a fruit, which is protected by the leaves.*

## GREEN CARPET

Tiny floating plants, such as duckweeds (*right*), often carpet the water surface like grass on a lawn. Here they do not compete for light with submerged waterweeds or algae. Duckweeds are among the world's smallest and simplest flowering plants. Tiny roots hang down from the leaves and absorb minerals from the water, and so duckweeds can grow in water that is too deep for plants that need to be rooted on the bottom.

## LEAF SHAPES

Some water plants, such as water crowfoot (*left*), have two types of leaves – large, flat leaves that float on the surface, and finely divided leaves under the surface. The fine, submerged leaves offer less resistance to the current of fast-flowing rivers and streams. The leaves that float on the surface are good at catching the sunlight the plants need.

## MEAT-EATING PLANTS

To help them survive in the poor soil of bogs and marshes, carnivorous plants trap insects and other small animals to get extra nutrients. The yellow trumpet pitcher plant (*right*) of the southeastern United States attracts insects with a glistening yellow-green hood covered with nectar glands. Insects fall down into the pitcher, where they are dissolved by digestive juices into a soupy meal. The plant absorbs its meal, full of nutrients, through the walls of the pitcher.

## FLOWER FLAG

Like most water plants, yellow flag (*left*), also known as yellow iris, produces its flowers above the water surface. It is pollinated by bumblebees, which crawl right inside the flower, following lines called honey guides on the petals. These point the way to the nectar. As the bee crawls into the flower, it deposits the pollen it is carrying from other yellow flags onto the stigma, or female part of the flower. As the bee climbs out of the flower, it collects a new load of pollen from the anthers, or male part of the flower. The stigma curls out of the way to avoid receiving its own pollen.

# PEAT BOGS

**L**arge areas in cooler parts of the world consist of soggy, flat land with peaty soil. These mires, as such habitats are called, include bogs and fens and are found particularly often in Canada, Russia, and most of Europe, especially Finland. Peat forms when dead plant material only partly decomposes in waterlogged soil. This can happen on the edge of a lake or on higher ground where rainfall is heavy and rocks are hard and acidic. A bog may take thousands of years to form. In contrast to acidic bogs, fens are fed by groundwater as well as rainfall and tend to have neutral or even alkaline peat. Few plants can tolerate the acidic conditions of bogs, but carnivorous plants, cotton sedges, and cranberries are common. Waterlogged bogs are ideal places for aquatic insects and biting flies, which provide food for birds and frogs. Many birds nest in bogs, among them snipes, redshanks, curlews, plovers, and divers. Hunting birds range from spectacular merlins and hobbies to short-eared owls and golden eagles.

## VACUUM CLEANERS

Bladderworts have small bladders, or sacs, on their thin, feathery underwater leaves. If aquatic insects brush against trigger hairs on the bladders, a trapdoor snaps open. Water is sucked into the bladder, carrying the insect with it (*above*). The bladderwort's trap works rather like a botanical vacuum cleaner.

## MIRACLE MOSS

The most characteristic peat bog plant is sphagnum, commonly called peat moss (*left*). This amazing bright green, bushy moss soaks up water like a huge bath sponge. It can absorb up to ten times its own weight in water. In the past it was used to dress soldiers' wounds, and American Indians used dried sphagnum as diapers for babies. Today, it is used by gardeners to line hanging baskets and stop water from draining away too quickly. Sphagnum sucks nutrients out of the water, and in peat bogs it makes the water even more acidic and poor in nutrients.

## BOG BIRDS

Many waders, such as curlews (*right*), nest in bogs because there they can find plenty of safe nesting sites and insects to eat. The mother and young are both well camouflaged to blend in with the vegetation, and the fluffy chicks can run as soon as they hatch. Birds also use peat bogs as winter resting places or feeding areas during migration journeys.

## STICKY FLYPAPER

A fly provides a tasty snack and a welcome source of extra nutrients for this sundew plant (*left*). Special hairs on the leaves have sticky droplets on their ends. Insects are attracted to the glistening droplets and stick to the leaves like flies on flypaper. As the fly struggles, the leaf folds around it, and hairs pour digestive juices over the flys body. The plant can then absorb nutrients from the fly's body. After a day or so, all that is left of the fly is a dry, empty husk. The leaf straightens out again, ready to catch its next meal.

## HOW A PEAT BOG FORMS

A peat bog may form when a lake fills in with mud and plants.

*The water is clear, with mud on the bottom of the lake.*

*Silt and mud collect around plant roots. This buildup allows plants to grow across the lake.*

*Mosses grow, die, and start to rot, building up layers of peat.*

*Bog mosses build up domes of peat above the level of the water. This is called a raised bog.*

## BOG BODIES

Over 1,000 ancient bodies (*left*) have been found preserved in peat bogs in Britain, Scandinavia, and northern Germany. The acid conditions and low levels of oxygen in the bogs prevented the bodies from decomposing. Oxygen is required for decomposition to occur because the bacteria that break down plant and animal material need oxygen to survive. Acidic peat is such a good preservative that it is possible to identify the last meal of a 2,000-year-old body unearthed from the peat.

# RIVER ANIMALS

As a river flows from the mountains to the sea, its moving water provides a variety of places for animals to feed and shelter. Insect larvae, worms, water snails, and shrimps living on the riverbed are snapped up by hungry fish, crayfish, and turtles. The fish are, in turn, hunted by otters, crocodiles, and birds such as herons, dippers, and kingfishers. Swallows and bats swoop low over the water to scoop up insects hatching from the water's surface. The moving water of rivers holds much more oxygen for animals to breathe than the still water of ponds and lakes. River animals, however, must avoid being washed away by the current or smashed against the rocks. They hide away in crevices, glue themselves to rocks, or cling tightly with hooks and suckers. In some rivers muddy water may make it difficult for animals to navigate or catch food. Some animals, such as salmon and eels, spend only part of their life cycle in rivers, moving to the sea to breed or feed.

Caddis flies, mayflies, and stone flies are common in upper rivers.

Trout like the oxygen here and can swim strongly against the current.

Otters and water voles (water rats) make nests in the middle river.

Kingfishers feed on fish, such as pike, carp, and bream.

Estuaries teem with worms, shellfish, and crustaceans.

**THE UPPER RIVER**
Fast-flowing water contains plenty of oxygen but few plants for animals to eat.

**THE MIDDLE RIVER**
Here the river is wider, with a smooth layer of mud and silt covering the riverbed. Plants take root along the riverbanks.

**THE LOWER RIVER**
When the river flows into the sea, it slows down and deposits mud and silt to form an estuary.

## SPECTACULAR SALMON

Salmon make long migration journeys from their feeding grounds in the sea to their breeding grounds in rivers. They usually return to the river where they themselves hatched, recognizing the distinctive smell of the water. As they journey upriver, the salmon may have to leap up waterfalls (*right*). They make their best jumps from deep water because they can build up speed beforehand. Many jumps fail, though, and the salmon may drop back exhausted.

## LIFE IN THE FAST LANE

A leech (*left*) has two suckers, which it uses to cling to stones or water plants so it is not swept away by the current. Other adaptations to life in fast-flowing waters include the hooks of blackfly larvae and the flattened bodies of crayfish, flatworms, stone fly nymphs, and mayfly nymphs. Some caddis fly larvae make cases around their bodies and stick themselves to stones or weigh their cases down with pebbles.

## FLYING UNDERWATER

The dipper (*right*) has the remarkable ability to walk underwater up the beds of fast-flowing streams as it searches for water insects, tadpoles, and worms. Its tail acts as a hydroplane in the current to keep its feet firmly on the bottom. The bird also dives into the water from the air. The dipper is a good indicator that water is clean. If pollution kills the insects that it feeds on, the dipper cannot survive.

## STREAMLINED HUNTER

The shy and inquisitive otter (*below*) is a land animal that spends much of its time in the water, particularly when feeding. Its fur is waterproof. An otter hunts for eels, trout, and crayfish from dusk to dawn, detecting its prey by sight or using its whiskers to sense vibrations made by fish as they swim. For slow swimming, the otter moves its webbed feet in a dog paddle. For greater speed, the otter holds its legs close to the body and flexes its whole body up and down. The flattened tail acts as a rudder.

# LAKE AND POND DWELLERS

The still waters of lakes and ponds are complex and delicate ecosystems, where the balance of living things changes with the seasons, the climate, and the water levels. These ecosystems are easily upset by pollution, including increased nutrient levels from sewage and fertilizers, which encourage the growth of algae that block out the light and use up oxygen. In a clean pond or lake there are three main zones: the pelagic zone of deep, open water in the middle, with algae, plankton, and fish; the benthic, or bottom, zone, with algae, worms, larvae, and mollusks living in or on the mud; and the rich and varied littoral zone around the edge, with reeds and other rooted plants, together with a host of animals. Deeper lakes usually contain fewer animals than shallow ones but a greater variety of species. Lakes and ponds may freeze over in the winter, but the wildlife survive in a layer of cold water trapped under the ice.

## FEATHERED FISHERMAN

The large and powerful great blue heron (*left*) of North America often stands motionless at the edge of ponds and lakes watching for fish or frogs to come within reach. It may also stalk its prey, eventually spearing its catch with its long, sharp bill or using the bill like a pair of pincers to hold its prey. Most of these herons migrate south to warmer places in the winter.

## DIVING BELL

The European water spider (*right*) is the only spider to spend virtually its whole life underwater. It cannot take in oxygen from the water, though, so it lives inside a bell-shaped web of silk, which it fills with air. It takes up to six trips to and from the surface to fill the silken bell with air. Once the diving bell is finished, the spider eats, mates, and lays its eggs inside. It leaves the bell only to catch food.

## FILTERING FLAMINGOS

Flamingos (*right*) wade into salty lakes to filter algae, small plants, and animals from the water. They trap the food particles with comblike plates on their bill. Flamingos live in large colonies, sometimes containing thousands of birds. They form a spectacular, but smelly, sea of pink on lakes such as Lake Nakuru in East Africa.

## WOOD DUCK

The beautiful iridescent colors of the male wood duck (*left*) contrast sharply with the camouflaged grays and browns of the female. Wood ducks live in lakes and ponds in wooded areas and nest in tree cavities or nest boxes. Soon after hatching, the young jump from the nest cavity down to the ground and follow their mother to the water.

## UNIQUE SPECIES

Lakes are often home to unique species that develop in isolation, cut off from others of their kind. Lake Victoria and Lake Tanganyika in East Africa are home to hundreds of different species of cichlid fish, such as these (*right*) guarding their nest from a terrapin. The different species can live together because they are adapted to eating different kinds of food.

## POND MAKER

Beavers (*right*) create a pond around their home, called a lodge, by constructing a dam of sticks and stones across a river. The animals know instinctively how to build the dam, which may be as tall as a person and up to 330 feet (100 m) long. A beaver's pond is like a moat around a castle, helping to keep away predators, such as wolves and bears. A beaver can also use its pond to float logs and branches to the lodge and the dam.

## LOUDMOUTH GATORS

The largest reptiles in North America, alligators are also the loudest, with the males bellowing particularly loudly in the breeding season. The sound carries for long distances, warning other males to keep away and telling females where they are. Alligators in the Everglades dig large holes, which fill with water to provide a vital source for wildlife in the dry season. Alligators feed on the wildlife, such as turtles (*left*) and fish, sheltering in their gator holes.

## PRECIOUS PANTHER

Southern Florida is the last known refuge in the eastern United States for the puma, or cougar – known in the area as the Florida panther (*right*). This beautiful predator is a powerful and expert hunter, capable of jumping up to 20 feet (6 m) in a single bound. The Florida panther needs a large territory in which to hunt mammals, such as deer. Although the Everglades is big, it may not be big enough to save the species. There are probably only about 50-70 animals left in the wild.

## RARE EGRET

The reddish egret (*left*) hunts fish, frogs, and crabs in the shallow waters of Florida Bay at low tide. It lurches, twists, and turns through the water, dashing to the left and right in pursuit of its prey. Egrets, herons, and ibises were hunted in the 1880s to supply feathers for the hat trade. Decades later the birds were once again threatened as a result of destruction of their nesting and feeding areas and changes in water levels.

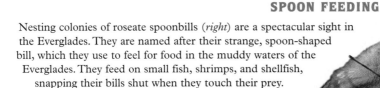

## SPOON FEEDING

Nesting colonies of roseate spoonbills (*right*) are a spectacular sight in the Everglades. They are named after their strange, spoon-shaped bill, which they use to feel for food in the muddy waters of the Everglades. They feed on small fish, shrimps, and shellfish, snapping their bills shut when they touch their prey.

# THE EVERGLADES

At the southern tip of Florida is a vast area of cypress swamp, mangroves, and marsh called the Everglades. This famous wetland covers a huge area – the portion preserved in Everglades National Park occupies some 2,358 sq miles (6,107 sq km) – yet is only just above sea level. In the summer, higher water levels allow animals to move freely through the park. In the winter, they gather around the few remaining water holes. More than 400 species of birds, 25 mammals, and 60 types of amphibians and reptiles can be found in the Everglades. The birds feed on various insects and fish that live in this warm, humid environment. Several rare animals have taken refuge in the Everglades, but the park is threatened on all sides by agriculture, drainage projects, buildings, and people.

UNITED STATES

THE EVERGLADES

## MUDDY MANGROVES

Where the Everglades meets the sea, the coasts are fringed with mangrove swamps. Mangroves are remarkable trees that are adapted to live in wet, salty places. Breathing pores in their roots take in oxygen from the air and help them survive in waterlogged mud with little oxygen. Red mangroves like these (*right*) protect the coast from storms and strong waves. They trap mud with their roots, and new areas of land build up around them.

## NESTING PREDATOR

The fish-eating osprey (*right*) is a conspicuous resident of the Everglades. Its bulky stick nest is built on dead trees, floating buoys, and telephone poles in the Florida Bay area or the mangrove wilderness. Ospreys are well adapted for catching fish, with sharp spines on their feet to catch hold of their slippery prey. They plunge feetfirst into the water, grasping the fish with their strong talons.

# MARSHES AND SWAMPS

The difference between a marsh and a swamp is that a marsh is a wet grassland, while a swamp is a waterlogged forest with specially adapted trees, such as swamp cypress or mangroves. These extraordinary half-worlds – part land, part water – are usually associated with the edges of lakes, reservoirs, ponds, rivers, and oceans where the waters become clogged with mud and a tangled, smelly mass of rotting plant and animal debris. Aquatic worms and crabs plough through the soft, slushy mud, and water snails graze on the stems and leaves of water plants. The shallow, protected waters of swamps and marshes provide ideal nurseries for baby fish, tadpoles, insect larvae, and the young of shellfish and shrimps. They are also an important feeding and breeding area for waterbirds, reptiles, and mammals. Swampy areas act as natural reservoirs, collecting and holding water in the rainy season and releasing it during the dry season.

### STRIPY SWIMMER

A few hundred Bengal tigers (*right*) live in the Sundarbans, an enormous soggy mangrove swamp on the western edge of the Ganges, Brahmaputra, and Meghna river deltas in Bangladesh and India. Dotted through the swamp are dozens of muddy islands covered with tropical forest, much of it submerged at high tide. The Sundarbans tigers hunt swamp deer, pigs, fish, and crabs and share their swamp with a rich variety of animals, including crocodiles and monkeys.

### SWAMP STORKS

The magnificent saddle-bill (*left*) is Africa's largest stork. It is named after the yellow "saddle" on its upper bill. The long, pointed bill makes a formidable weapon for stabbing fish and other prey in the water. The stork's big feet disturb the fish as it wades through the water.

## SUMMER SIESTA

Some lungfish (*right*) survive drought by going into a type of summer hibernation called estivation. As the water level falls, the fish burrows into the soft mud and secretes a mucous cocoon around its body. The cocoon stops moisture from evaporating from the fish's body, and the lungfish breathes air with its lungs through a porous lid of mud that seals the cocoon. During estivation, the body processes slow down so the lungfish uses very little energy. Some lungfish have survived up to four years of drought.

## AIR PLANTS

Hanging from the trees like long hair, Spanish moss (*left*) is one of the best-known air plants in the Everglades swamp of Florida. Although air plants, called epiphytes, grow on other plants, they are nonparasitic because they take their nourishment from the air. Despite its name, Spanish moss is a member of the pineapple family – the bromeliads. There are also rare epiphytic orchids in the Everglades as well as epiphytic vines and ferns.

## SCARCE SWALLOWTAIL

In Britain, the lovely swallowtail butterfly (*right*) survives only in a man-made marsh, the Norfolk Broads, created by the flooding of old peat excavations, which were worked in the Middle Ages. Land drainage has made the butterfly a rare species. The swallowtail caterpillars eat milk parsley plants, which vary in number each year. Many caterpillars are eaten by spiders, birds, and small mammals. Maintenance of high water levels in the broads and preservation of milk parsley are essential for the swallowtail's future survival.

## WATER WALKER

Unlike small insects that really do walk on water, the African jacana, or lily-trotter (*above*), cheats by walking over floating lily pads instead. Its big feet, with their long, thin toes, work like the long legs of water striders. They spread out the weight of the lily-trotter over a wide area and keep it from sinking down into the water.

# WATERY MOVEMENT

Many small water creatures just float or drift through the water, pushed along by the wind or water currents. Fish, frogs, water beetles, and other larger animals use their muscles to propel themselves along. Water is much denser than air, so it supports an animal's weight but also holds the animal back as it tries to swim along. To make swimming easier, aquatic animals have a smooth, streamlined shape, a slippery surface, and often webbed feet. Between the water and the air there is a thin invisible "skin," like a springy, bouncy platform. This forms on the surface of the water because water molecules are more attracted to each other than they are to the air above them, and they stick tightly together. Walkers on this surface skin – for example, water striders – have special adaptations, such as waxy feet to repel the water, and long legs to spread their weight.

### FROGGY PADDLE

At the first sign of danger, an adult frog will leap into the water (*left*). It can move faster through water than it can on land, and there are plenty of places to hide among the water plants. The long, slim body of a frog and its rounded snout make it a streamlined shape that can easily cut through the water. Its webbed back feet are like the flippers people wear when snorkeling or diving. The webbed feet push a lot of water out of the way at each stroke so the frog can swim fast.

## UNDERWATER TANK

Looking rather like a giant underwater tank, the hippopotamus (*left*) lumbers along the bottoms of rivers, lakes, and swamps. It is an excellent swimmer and diver and can stay underwater for up to five minutes. Hippos spend most of the daytime in the water because their skin loses water at a very high rate in air and they would rapidly dehydrate in the hot African sun. The animals are well adapted for an aquatic life. Water flows easily over their smooth skin, their webbed toes act like paddles, and they can close their nostrils and ears to keep the water out when they are underwater.

## HAIRY OARS

Water boatmen (*right*) live in ponds, canals, and ditches. These bugs have a streamlined, boat-shaped body and long, powerful back legs, which stick out of the sides of the body like oars. Hairs on the legs create a large surface area for brushing the water aside as the insect rows through the water.

## BLUE JEWEL

Kingfishers (*left*) are shy birds, usually seen as a swift flash of bright blue speeding like an arrow along a river bank. To catch fish, the kingfisher dives headfirst into the water from a perch. Sometimes it will hover before diving. Once in the water (*right*), the bird spears its prey in its daggerlike beak and holds it firmly until it gets back to the perch. There it beats its prey against a hard surface and swallows it headfirst. This makes sure the fish's fins and scales do not get caught in the bird's throat.

## EUROPEAN FOOD CHAIN

**ALGAE**

↓

**WATER FLEA**

↓

**STICKLEBACK**

↓

**PERCH**

↓

**HERON**

*Fish-eating waterbirds such as herons, kingfishers, and storks are often the top predators at the end of wetland food chains. These food chains, however, often include more than one fish – big fish gobbling up smaller ones.*

### MASKED BANDIT

Mischievous raccoons use their long, mobile fingers to find and catch aquatic prey, such as crayfish, fish, frogs, and clams. They naturally tend to rub, feel, and dunk their food in water, perhaps to investigate their prey or get rid of nasty skin secretions. Raccoons are more active in the evening than in the daytime and are good swimmers and climbers. The name raccoon comes from *arahkunem*, a Native American (Algonquian) name for the animal. It means, "He who scratches with his hands."

# PREDATORS AND PREY

Wetlands are full of tasty meals for predators to eat, especially water insects and fish. The biggest predators include alligators, crocodiles, anacondas, tigers, and fish eagles. Some predators, such as snakes and otters, hunt in the water. Others, such as bats and fish eagles, swoop down to snatch a meal from the water's surface. Different techniques for catching prey include the surprise ambush of a crocodile, the high-speed chase of an otter, the stealthy stalk of a tiger, and the tricky trap of a Venus flytrap plant. Mammals, such as otters and bats, together with reptiles, such as alligators and snakes, tend to hunt under cover of darkness. Birds, however, are daytime hunters. To catch and kill their prey, wetland predators rely on weapons such as sharp bills, teeth, and talons, as well as poison and electric shock.

### SHOOTING INSECTS

The remarkable archerfish (*left*) spits drops of water up from the surface of the water to shoot down insects sitting on leaves above. If the insect falls into the water, the archerfish can snap it up. If the fish is only an inch or two from the insect, it will jump out of the water and snatch the insect with its jaws rather than shoot it down.

## FISHING EAGLE

The national bird of the United States, the bald eagle (*right*) is a versatile predator of fish, birds, and small mammals. It swoops down to the water surface to snatch fish in its strong, spiny talons. Groups of bald eagles gather at salmon spawning grounds in Alaska, where the large number of exhausted and dead fish provide easy meals. This magnificent eagle is named after the white feathers on its head – an old meaning of the word "bald."

## FISHING SPIDER

Sitting on floating leaves or twigs with their front legs resting on the surface of the water, fishing spiders (*left*) lie in wait for their prey. Hairs on their legs detect ripples in the water caused by fish swimming nearby. The spider can determine the position of a fish from the direction of the ripples and the distance between them. It kills its prey with a poisonous bite.

## PRISON BARS

The Venus flytrap (*below*) is the most spectacular hunting plant, living only in a patch of marshy country in North and South Carolina. Insects are attracted to the trap by its color or the sweet nectar below the spikes. If they brush against special trigger hairs on the surface of the trap, the two halves snap shut in a third of a second or less. The walls of the trap press tightly together and digestive juices dissolve the insect's body.

## NORTH AMERICAN FOOD CHAIN

**ALGAE**

**MOSQUITO LARVAE**

**BLUEGILL**

**FLORIDA SPOTTED GAR**

**ALLIGATOR**

*Wetland food chains rely on tiny algae and other photosynthetic organisms in the water, which provide food for a variety of water insects. These, in turn, feed fish, which are preyed on by larger predators such as alligators and snakes.*

# DEFENSE

From armor and camouflage to poison and chemical weapons, wetland animals use a variety of strategies to stay alive. For shoals of fish, flocks of waterbirds, herds of antelope, or families of beavers there is safety in numbers. Many animals prefer to hide among the water plants, such as under lily pads or in between the reeds along the water's edge. The sitatunga, an African antelope, submerges itself under the water if it senses danger, with only the tip of its nose protruding above the surface. Frightening enemies away is another survival tactic. Some animals display colored markings, while snakes or crocodiles may hiss and puff up their bodies with air so they look bigger and more scary. Chemical weapons include acids sprayed by some caterpillars and poisons secreted by the skin of toads and salamanders. Coming out at night helps some creatures, such as eels and moths, to avoid their predators.

## FLASH COLORS

The fire-bellied toads of Europe and Asia have undersides that are boldly marked with blotches of bright red, orange, or yellow, but the tops of their bodies are camouflaged with gray or green colors (*above*). To startle a predator, the toads suddenly expose their bright colors, giving themselves time to escape. The bright belly colors warn of poisonous skin secretions

## THE NUMBERS GAME

By keeping together, the members of this shoal of minnows (*right*) can help one another spot danger. They also have less of a chance of being singled out for attack. Predators find shoals of fish confusing targets, and most of the fish escape an attack.

## CHAIN MAIL

The outside of a crocodile's or alligator's body is completely covered in tough scales and bony plates set into the thick, leathery skin (*left*). This coat of armor is rather like the coat of chain mail worn by medieval knights. Few predators will risk attacking a well-armored adult crocodile, with its sharp teeth and powerful jaws. Crocodiles' main enemy is people, who kill them for their skins, for food, or because they are dangerous.

## HARMLESS HOGNOSE

The hognose snake (*right*) of North America is harmless, but it makes itself look frightening to scare away predators. First it widens its neck into a cobra-type hood. Then it hisses loudly and strikes toward the enemy. If all *that* does not work, the hognose snake smears itself with smelly scent and then rolls over and pretends to be dead. Predators prefer to eat live prey, so they leave the hognose snake alone.

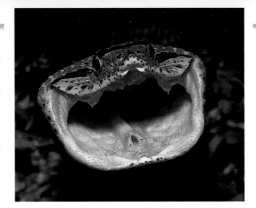

## CLEVER CAMOUFLAGE

Bitterns (*left*) build their nests among reeds or sedges where they are well hidden and protected from enemies. These shy and secretive birds are very difficult to see in their marsh and swamp habitat. When threatened, a bittern often "freezes" with its bill pointing straight up to the sky. The streaks on its breast feathers look just like reeds, and it may even sway back and forth like reeds in the wind.

## SHELL SECURITY

Water snails (*below*) can withdraw their body inside their hard shell for protection. The operculum, or door, to the shell can be closed to make a watertight seal. A snail's shell is secreted by a fold of the body wall called the mantle and is made largely of calcium salts taken in from the water. The large shell of the great pond snail needs a lot of calcium carbonate, so this species can thrive only in water containing plenty of lime, which is largely calcium.

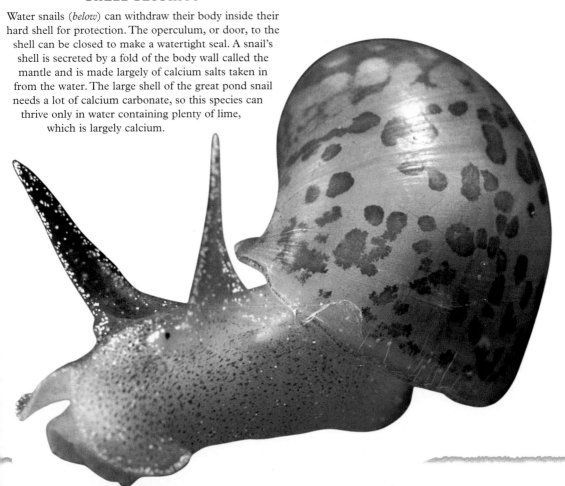

# NESTS, EGGS, AND YOUNG

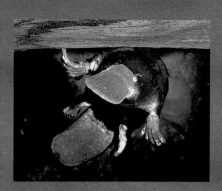

## PECULIAR PLATYPUS

The duck-billed platypus (*above*) is a very unusual mammal, unique to Australia, that lays eggs instead of giving birth to live young. The female lays (usually) two eggs at the end of a special breeding tunnel in a river bank, out of sight of predators. She curls herself around the eggs and incubates them for up to 14 days. The baby platypuses cut their way out of their eggs with an egg tooth. They feed on their mother's milk, which oozes out of her belly onto her fur.

The luxuriant plant growth of wetland habitats provides safe places for animals to lay eggs, build nests, and give birth, while the shallow water areas contain plenty of food for the young to eat, as well as calm water in which they can practice their swimming skills. Huge colonies of breeding birds, such as flamingos and herons, are found in wetlands. Some animals, such as dragonflies and frogs, spend part of their lives in the water and part on land. The eggs are laid in water and the young develop there, but the adults fly or move overland to new wetland areas. This helps avoid inbreeding in small populations and prevents chance disasters from wiping out whole populations.

## REED BASKET

The nest of the reed warbler, found in Europe and Asia, is a woven basket attached to dry reed stems above the wet reed bed (*left*). The nest is anchored with "handles," and both male and female birds add grass, feathers, and flowers on top to build up the nest. Reed warblers need considerable acrobatic skill because the reeds sway and wave in the wind.

## A DOUBLE LIFE

Struggling to pull itself free of its larval skin, an adult dragonfly is about to begin its life as a hunter in the air (*left*). Eventually, it will mate, and the female will lay her eggs in the water. The eggs hatch into nymphs, which live underwater for between one and five years. The nymphs breathe through gills on the tip of their abdomen and feed mainly on aquatic invertebrates. They shed their skins several times as they slowly grow into adults. This gradual change to an adult form without passing through a pupal stage is called incomplete metamorphosis.

## NESTING COUPLE

The male stickleback encourages a female to swim through his nest of waterweeds and lay her eggs (*above*). Then he will also swim through the nest and fertilize the eggs with his sperm. The male guards the nest closely, chasing away enemies and fanning a current of oxygen-rich water over the eggs with his front fins. Even after the young hatch, the male stickleback keeps watch over his family, picking up in his mouth any that stray too far away.

## FLAMINGO MILK

To make sure their chicks get enough food, flamingo parents (*left*) produce a rich "milk" in their upper digestive tract. The milk is bright red because it contains red pigment from the food the birds eat. Their feathers also become pink or red for the same reason. When chicks are hungry, they make begging calls. Their beaks are straight at first, and they have fluffy down feathers to keep them warm. Older chicks gather into a group called a crèche; adults take turns guarding the crèche and going off to feed.

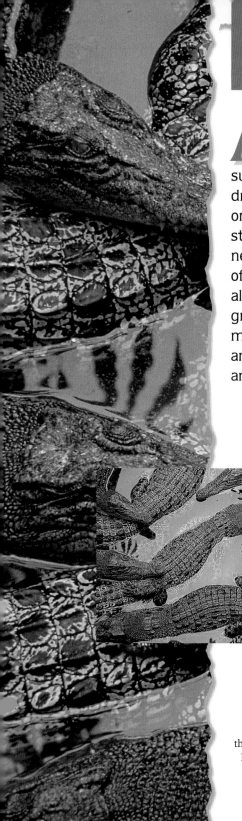

# LIVING TOGETHER

Animals living in a group help each other look out for danger and take care of their young. A large source of food can cause animals, such as crocodiles, to congregate together. A drought can force groups to gather at water holes or any remaining source of water. Herons, egrets, storks, and other wetland birds gather together to nest in large colonies. Other animals, such as shoals of fish or herds of antelope or horses, live together all year-round. Among mammals such as zebras, a group of females and their young may be led by a male. Other family groups in wetlands include otter and beaver families. Sometimes different kinds of animals live together and help each other to survive.

## CROCODILE GATHERINGS

Crocodiles (*left*) gather together in loose groups to bask in the sun, share food, court, and nest. Groups, called pods, of young crocodiles hang out together and warn each other of danger. In times of drought, crocodiles of all ages gather together to share the water and avoid competing for scarce resources. Dominant crocodiles defend territories, which contain mates, basking sites, feeding places, nests, and dens.

## PIRANHA PACKS

Packs of red-bellied piranhas (*right*) hunt in the tropical rivers of South America. In a matter of minutes they can strip the flesh off animals as large as goats that have accidentally fallen into the water. Meat-eating piranhas turn to eating meat only when plant food is hard to find. For most of the year they live on fruit and nuts that fall into the water.

## ZEBRA HERDS

Splashing across the Okavango swamplands in Africa, these Burchell's zebras (*right*) protect themselves from predators by sticking together. Zebras live in family groups made up of females and their young, led by a strong male. Rival males will fight each other for control of a herd of females. The zebras communicate by means of sounds or body language, such as moving the position of the ears or the tail. Several families share a home range and may join in large herds, but family members can always recognize each other by voice, scent, and stripe pattern.

## PLANT LODGERS

The pitcher plants of marshes and bogs sometimes have animal lodgers living inside their pitchers. This one (*left*) has a small tree frog sitting at the top, waiting to snap up insects before they fall down into the living trap. The twin-spurred pitcher has developed in its stem a small chamber that is regularly used by ants. As they steal a meal from the bottom of the pitcher, the ants accidentally help chop up the pitcher's food.

## HIPPO HERDS

During the day hippopotamuses stay in the water in groups of about 10 or 15, which may be all-male bachelor groups or nursery groups. The nursery groups contain females and their young within the territory of a dominant male bull. Some bulls are solitary. In the evenings the aquatic groups break up and the animals go ashore to feed. Other animals sometimes live with hippos, such as the oxpeckers feeding on tiny creatures on the skin of this hippo (*below*).

# PEOPLE AND WETLANDS

P eople use wetlands in many ways – for transportation, fishing, farming, tourism, recreation, and sport. The reeds from marshes are used for thatching or to make houses and boats, and peat bogs provide a source of fuel and garden soil. Transporting goods and people by water is still important in many parts of the world. Many people live near rivers and lakes and rely on them for their water supply. The energy from flowing water can be used to make electricity. The energy is called hydroelectric power – "hydro" means water. Unexpected floods can cause terrible problems for people living near rivers, such as the Mississippi in the United States or the Huang Ho (Yellow River) in China.

## CORMORANT FISHING

For centuries, cormorants have been used by people to help them catch fish (*below*). A ring is placed around the bird's neck to prevent it from swallowing the fish. When the cormorant comes to the surface, it is hauled to the boat on a special perch, and the fish is taken out of its mouth. Later, the ring is removed so the cormorant can feed itself. Experienced birds can be trained to fish without the ring.

## CROCODILE PEOPLE

The crocodile plays an important part in the myths and legends of the Iatmul people of the Sepik River in New Guinea. The saltwater crocodile was common in the mangrove swamps of the Sepik River basin and is believed by some peoples to be the creator of all living things. Its skull is kept in the men's spirit houses, such as this one (*left*), and the initiation ceremony for young men involves cutting their skin to look like the scales of a crocodile.

## PEAT CUTTING

These men (*right*) are cutting blocks of peat in Scotland's Outer Hebrides to burn for fuel. They are using a special spade with a long handle and a thin blade, but peat is also extracted with bulldozers and large mechanical excavators. Peat turfs cut by hand are turned and stacked to allow them to dry before they are used. Peat is used to supply soil for gardens as well as for fuel. In addition to affecting wildlife, the digging up of peat and its use as fuel leads to the release of the greenhouse gas carbon dioxide into the atmosphere, potentially contributing to global warming. Many scientists think that major fires in peat bogs, like large forest fires, may also feed significant amounts of carbon dioxide into the atmosphere.

## FLOODED FIELDS

In Asia, artificial wetlands are created when people flood fields to farm rice, which grows best when the plants are rooted in waterlogged mud. These flooded fields are called paddies and can also be used to farm frogs or fish, sometimes in pools next to the fields. This farmer (*left*) is herding his geese across a rice paddy. People have grown rice in Thailand, China, and India for at least five thousand years.

## BOAT TRAFFIC

Zooming through a swamp on an airboat (*right*) can be fun, but it disturbs the wildlife more than do boats without engines, such as canoes. The propellers from airboats can also injure wildlife, such as manatees in the Florida Everglades. Boat engines cause a lot of pollution and noise, and the wash from boats can drown the eggs and chicks of birds nesting in the vegetation on the water's edge.

# PROTECTING WETLANDS

France's Camargue
wetland is protected as a
national park and preserve
(*below*), but it remains
surrounded by industry
and cities. Pollution seeps
into the park wetlands,
and the presence of large
numbers of tourists may
frighten and disturb the
wildlife. Illegal hunting
also goes on in the park.
So, even though a wetland
may be officially protected,
it still has to be managed
very carefully, taking into
account problems caused
outside the protected area.

**W**etlands are special places for wildlife, supporting perhaps a tenth of all the world's species, by some estimates. They are useful to people in all sorts of ways and have a vital effect on the environment around them. Wetlands help control flooding by soaking up heavy rainfall and releasing it slowly. Mangrove swamps protect coasts from soil erosion and the effects of storms. In some places wetlands act as a form of natural pollution control, filtering the water that flows through them and removing impurities. On a global scale peat bogs "lock up" carbon dioxide released by burning coal and oil and so help reduce global warming. An estimated half of the world's wetlands were destroyed during the past century, and those that remain urgently need protection if they are to survive in the future. Leaving wetlands alone, however, is not enough, as many would just silt up and disappear. Careful control of wetlands' water supply, therefore, is important.

RESERVE NATIONALE DE CAMARGUE

DIGUE A LA MER (1860)

VOUS ENTREZ DANS LA RESERVE
NATIONALE DE CAMARGUE

NE QUITTEZ PAS LA DIGUE
RESPECTEZ LA NATURE

PHARE DE LA GACHOLLE    1 KM
ACCES A LA MER    4 KM
LES SAINTES MARIES    12 KM

## MINING PROBLEMS

The Ranger Uranium Mine (*left*) lies on the edge of Kakadu National Park in Australia's Northern Territory. Kakadu, recognized by the United Nations Educational, Scientific, and Cultural Organization (UNESCO) as a World Heritage Site, contains rivers, flood plains, creeks, and lakes called billabongs spread over a territory bigger than the land area of New Jersey. The park is home to many rare and unique species that are threatened by the presence of the mine.

## CLEANING UP WETLANDS

All over the world, people are cleaning up rivers, removing trash, and turning them into places that are pleasant to visit and safe for local wildlife. They are also making new wetlands, by digging ponds in their school playgrounds, gardens, or city parks. Even a small pond can be a vital refuge for wildlife, and the efforts of small groups of people (*right*) can make a difference.

## CAPTIVE BREEDING

This young alligator (*left*) has been raised in captivity on a farm and is being released into the wild. American alligators were once rare, but conservation measures, such as captive breeding and protection of their habitat, have increased their numbers.

## RIVER MANAGEMENT

People build dams across rivers to control flooding, provide a water supply, and generate electricity. A dam (*right*), however, changes the amount of water and sediment in a river, and a huge artificial lake is created behind the dam. There may not be enough water downstream for people, farms, plants, or animals. Changing the natural course of a river may actually cause flooding or other problems in the long term.

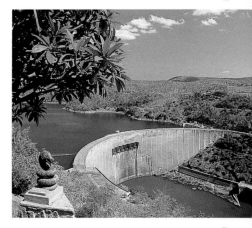

## RARE SPECIES

The Iberian, or Spanish, lynx (*left*) once occurred throughout Spain, but as of 2005 the total number of adults was estimated to be only about a hundred, living in two separate regions in southern Spain: the Coto Doñana National Park on the Atlantic and the Andújar and Cardeña nature parks in the Sierra Morena mountains. This beautiful lynx has been reduced to near extinction by rapid economic development, with roads and agriculture destroying its habitat. It is the world's most threatened cat species. Rare species like this can be protected through preservation of their habitat, elimination of trade in their fur or other body parts, and captive breeding programs.

# FOR FURTHER INFORMATION

*The followng are some of the sources available that can help you find out more about life in wetlands and inland waters, and about their conservation.*

**Books**

Campbell, Andrew. *Protecting Wetlands*. Protecting Habitats series (Gareth Stevens)
Dugan, Patrick (editor). *Guide to Wetlands* (Firefly)
Luhr, James F. (editor). *Smithsonian Earth* (DK Publishing)
Moore, Peter D., and Richard Garratt. *Wetlands*. Biomes of the Earth series (Facts on File)
Niering, William A. *Wetlands*. Audubon Society Nature Guides series (Knopf)
Reid, George K., and Sally D. Kaicher. *Pond Life*. Golden Guide series (St. Martin's Press)
Walker, Pam, and Elaine Wood. *The Saltwater Wetland*. Life in the Sea series (Facts on File)

**Web sites**

Discover Canada's Wetland Habitats (University of Guelph)
    **www.aquatic.uoguelph.ca/wetlands/wetlandframes.htm**
Everglades Ecosystem (U.S. National Park Service) **www.nps.gov/ever/eco/**
Missouri Botanical Garden **mbgnet.net/fresh/wetlands/index.htm**
Ramsar Convention on Wetlands **www.ramsar.org/**
U.S. Environmental Protection Agency **www.epa.gov/owow/wetlands/**
U.S. Fish and Wildlife Service, National Wetlands Inventory **www.fws.gov/nwi/**

**Publisher's note to educators and parents:** Our editors have carefully reviewed these Web sites to ensure that they are suitable for children. Many Web sites change frequently, however, and we cannot guarantee that a site's future contents will continue to meet our high standards of quality and educational value. Be advised that children should be closely supervised whenever they access the Internet.

**Museums and parks**

American Museum of Natural History
Central Park West at 79th Street
New York, NY 10024

Greater St. Lucia Wetland Park
St. Lucia
KwaZulu-Natal
South Africa

National Museum of Natural History
10th Street and Constitution Avenue, NW
Washington, DC 20560

North Carolina Museum of
    Natural Sciences
11 West Jones Street
Raleigh, NC 27601

Olentangy River Wetland Research Park
Ohio State University
352 Dodridge Road
Columbus, OH 43202

Ontario Science Centre
770 Don Mills Road
Toronto ON M3C 1T3
Canada

Wetlands Institute
1075 Stone Harbor Boulevard
Stone Harbor, NJ 08247

Wildlife Experience
10035 South Peoria
Parker, CO 80134

# GLOSSARY

**algae:** a group of simple plants that carry out photosynthesis and range from tiny microorganisms to huge seaweeds; the singular form of *algae* is *alga*

**bacteria:** a group of single-celled microbes that lack a distinct cell nucleus

**carnivore:** a creature that normally eats mainly animal tissue

**crustaceans:** a group of animals that have a hard exoskeleton around their body, which consists of segments and has jointed limbs and two pairs of antennae; most live in water – among them barnacles, crabs, lobsters, and shrimps

**echolocation:** a method used by some animals, such as dolphins, to detect the presence of objects; it makes use of echoes of sounds made by the animal and is similar to the underwater sonar system used by ships

**ecosystem:** a group of interdependent living things along with the environment they inhabit; a pond and the organisms living in it form an ecosystem

**estuary:** the broad stretch of a river where it flows into the sea or ocean, and freshwater and salt water mix

**food chain:** a series of organisms that depend on each other for food

**larva:** a young form of an animal; larvae (as the plural form is spelled) tend to be quite different from adults in form – for example, the larva of a moth or butterfly is a caterpillar

**mangrove:** a type of tree or shrub supported by a tangle of aerial roots

**mollusks:** a group of animals that are invertebrates (lacking a backbone) and have a soft body, a muscular foot, and, often, a hard shell – such as snails

**nymph:** a larva of certain insects; the nymph looks somewhat similar to an adult and does not pass through a pupa stage as it matures

**photosynthesis:** a sunlight-based process used by green plants and some microorganisms to make water and carbon dioxide into food

**plankton:** very tiny organisms – including plants, animals, and bacteria – found in a body of water

**predator:** an organism that kills other organisms (called "prey") for food

**pupa:** a stage in the development of certain insects, during which larvae are transformed into adults; insects in the pupal stage typically lie within a cocoon or similar protective case

**reptiles:** a group of vertebrates that are cold-blooded, have dry skin, and use lungs to breathe; they include crocodiles, lizards, snakes, and turtles

**shellfish:** a general word for creatures that live in water, have a shell, and are eaten by humans, such as many crustaceans and mollusks

**shoal:** a large group, or "school," of marine creatures, such as a shoal of fish

**tundra:** a type of landscape in polar regions featuring shrubs, mosses, plants, and the like; the ground is permanently frozen there, and trees cannot grow

# INDEX